JAMAICA

Simon Scoones
with photographs by David Cumming

The Bookwright Press
New York · 1992

Our Country

Australia
Canada
China
France
Greece
India
Italy
Jamaica
Japan
The Netherlands
Spain
The United Kingdom
West Germany

Cover *The Blue Lagoon,
near Port Antonio, is one of
the most beautiful bays on
Jamaica's north coast.*

First published in the
United States in 1992 by
The Bookwright Press
387 Park Avenue South
New York, NY 10016

First published in 1992 by
Wayland (Publishers) Ltd
61 Western Road, Hove
East Sussex BN3 1JD, England

© Copyright 1992 Wayland (Publishers) Ltd

Library of Congress Cataloging-in-Publication Data

Scoones, Simon.
    Jamaica/by Simon Scoones.
      p.   cm. — (Our country)
    Includes bibliographical references and index.
    Summary: Introduces the geography, weather, industry, and
culture of Jamaica.
    ISBN 0-531-18419-6
    1. Jamaica—Juvenile literature. [1. Jamaica.]   I. Title.
II. Series: Our country (New York, N.Y.)
F1868.2.S35 1992
972.92—dc20   91-39126
                                    CIP
                                    AC

Typeset by Dorchester Typesetting Group Ltd
Printed in Italy by Rotolito Lombarda S.p.A.

All words printed in **bold** are
explained in the glossary on
page 30.

Contents

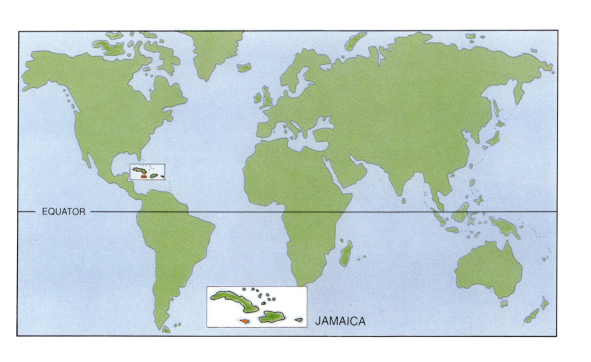

EQUATOR

JAMAICA

We live in Jamaica

Jamaica is an island of beautiful beaches and mountains in the Caribbean Sea. About a third of the people live in Kingston, the **capital**. Fewer live in the central part of Jamaica because it has so many mountains.

The first people to live in Jamaica were the Arawak Indians. Their name for the island was "Xaymaca," which means land of woods and water. That is how Jamaica got its name.

Settlers from European countries came to live on the island, and they brought over people from Africa to work on their **plantations**. So Jamaicans nowadays come from many different backgrounds.

In this book, twelve Jamaican children will tell you about their lives.

Kingston has a busy center, where many people go to work or shop.

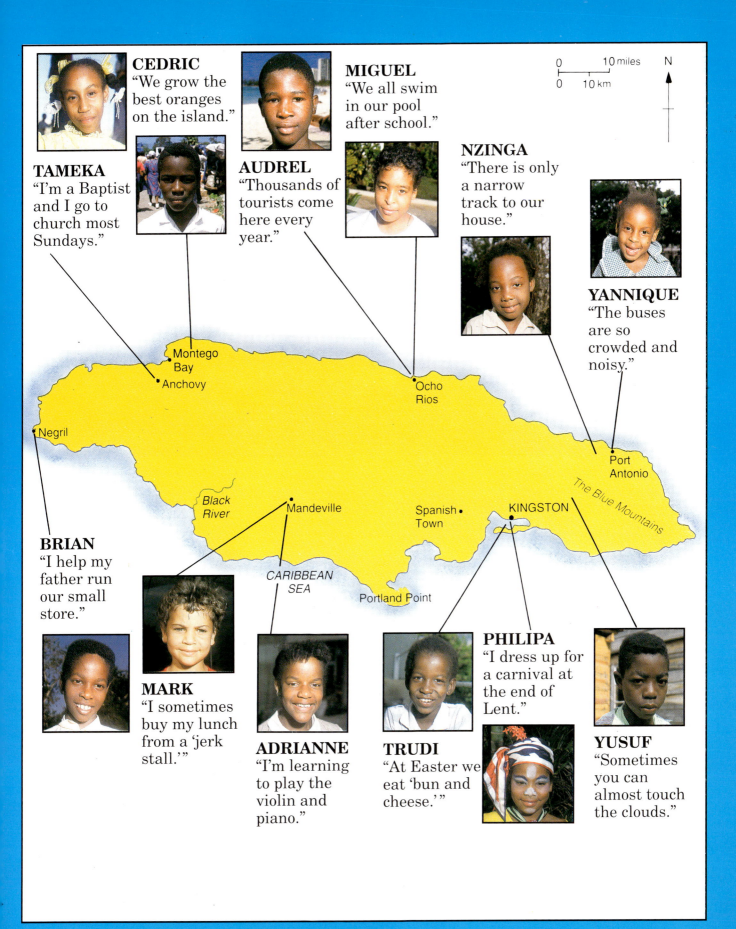

CEDRIC
"We grow the best oranges on the island."

TAMEKA
"I'm a Baptist and I go to church most Sundays."

MIGUEL
"We all swim in our pool after school."

AUDREL
"Thousands of tourists come here every year."

NZINGA
"There is only a narrow track to our house."

YANNIQUE
"The buses are so crowded and noisy."

BRIAN
"I help my father run our small store."

MARK
"I sometimes buy my lunch from a 'jerk stall.'"

ADRIANNE
"I'm learning to play the violin and piano."

TRUDI
"At Easter we eat 'bun and cheese.'"

PHILIPA
"I dress up for a carnival at the end of Lent."

YUSUF
"Sometimes you can almost touch the clouds."

0   10 miles
0   10 km
N

Montego Bay
Anchovy
Negril
Ocho Rios
Port Antonio
The Blue Mountains
Black River
Mandeville
CARIBBEAN SEA
Spanish Town
KINGSTON
Portland Point

The weather

Jamaica is a **tropical** island. It is very warm all year round because the sun is directly overhead. The driest and sunniest months are from November to April, which is when lots of **tourists** come to Jamaica to escape the bad weather in their own countries.

The island is cooled by winds that blow off the sea. Jamaicans call these winds "Dr. Breeze." It is coolest on the higher land in the middle of the island. In the late summer, **hurricanes** can sometimes sweep across the island, causing a lot of damage. In 1988 Hurricane Gilbert destroyed thousands of homes and killed forty-five people.

The weather in Jamaica can change very quickly. One minute it is sunny, and the next it is pouring with rain.

It rains a lot in October and May. During the rest of the year there are sometimes short tropical downpours. During a downpour, the roads look more like rivers. But farmers are pleased because the rain waters the land and helps their crops grow.

"Sometimes you can almost touch the clouds."

"My name is Yusuf. My home is in the Blue Mountains near Kingston. It's cooler than in the rest of Jamaica, and we get more rain than places on the coast. Sometimes you can almost touch the clouds, they're so low."

"It's hot all year round."

"My name is Nzinga. That's me sitting on the left. I live in a small village just outside Port Antonio. Our school has open sides because the weather is hot all year round here. We finish school in the early afternoon, because it gets too hot to work."

Farming

The weather and soil are good for farming in Jamaica. Lots of farms are small, but people grow many different vegetables and fruit. Bananas are grown because they can be **harvested** all year round. Coconuts are grown to eat and to make into soap.

In the mountains, it is too steep and rocky to use tractors, so farmers do the work by hand. In the Blue Mountains near Kingston the rich soil is good for growing coffee beans.

In the low-lying, flat areas there are very large farms called plantations. These were started when Jamaica was ruled by the

On sugar plantations most of the work is now done by machines, instead of by hand.

"Ours are the biggest and juiciest oranges on the whole island."

"My name is Cedric and I live in a village near Montego Bay. We grow oranges, which my mother sells in the market in town. I usually help to pick them, and here I am helping her at the market. Ours are the biggest and juiciest oranges on the whole island."

"Our coffee is the best in the world."

"I am Yusuf. We grow coffee at our home in the Blue Mountains. It grows as berries on bushes like this one. We pick the berries by hand when they turn red. Many people say our coffee is the best in the world. It costs a lot of money."

British, to grow crops that could not be grown in Britain, such as sugar cane.

Along the coast, fishing is important. A lot of the fish is sold to hotels and restaurants.

Industry and jobs

When bauxite is mined, big lumps of rock are dug right out of the ground.

Many people are leaving their jobs on farms to find work in the tourist industry. The number of vacationers in Jamaica has grown each year. They come to visit the beautiful beaches and swim in the warm sea. Tourism provides jobs in hotels, transportation and entertainment. Jamaicans also earn money making **souvenirs**, like jewelry made from **coral**, straw hats and bamboo baskets.

Rum is a popular drink that is made in Jamaica. It is made from a brown syrup called molasses, which comes from sugar cane. In factories the molasses is treated so the sugar turns into alcohol to make rum.

"I help my father to run our small store."

"My name is Brian. I live in Negril, on the west coast. Here I am with my father and sister in our small store. Dad runs the store while my mother takes care of the tourists in our guest house at the back."

"Thousands of tourists come here every year."

"My name is Audrel. My home is in Ocho Rios, on the north coast. Thousands of tourists come here every year to spend their vacations on our beautiful, sandy beaches. Lots of local people work in the hotels and restaurants here."

Jamaica also has a lot of an orange-colored rock called **bauxite**. The rock can be processed to make the metal, aluminum. Bauxite is **mined** using big machines. It is taken by truck to the ports where it is shipped abroad.

Schools

By law, children in Jamaica have to go to school until they are fourteen years old. School is free, but parents have to pay for the school uniform. Children learn English, math and science as well as other subjects. When they are eleven, they have to take an exam before moving to secondary school.

Most schools start at 7:30 in the morning and finish at 2:00 in the afternoon. It is too hot to learn very well in the afternoon hours. After school, many children have jobs to do as well as their homework. They may have to look after a younger brother or

These school children have just finished their classes and are going outside to play.

sister. In the countryside they may have to weed or plant seeds in the fields. Some children have to get up at 5:00 in the morning because they have to walk a long way to school.

"I'm five so I'm still in kindergarten."

"I'm called Yannique. Here I am at my school in Port Antonio. I'm only five years old so I'm still in kindergarten. I started here when I was three and I will leave it when I am six. Today I'm learning to write my name."

"It's less crowded than a school run by the government."

"My name is Miguel. I go to a private school in Ocho Rios. It's less crowded than schools run by the government. There are about 250 children here. They are from three to eleven years old. Our classes begin at 9:00 in the morning and end at 2:00 in the afternoon."

Religion

At this church service, the man in the water is being baptized.

There are many religions in Jamaica because it has such a mixture of people from different backgrounds and **cultures**. In all religions in Jamaica, music and singing are very important.

Most religious people in Jamaica are **Christians**. They go to different churches, including **Baptist** and **Roman Catholic**. They always wear their best clothes on Sundays and other holy days, when the churches are packed with people.

Other religions in Jamaica originally came from Africa. Rastafarianism is a modern religion that believes in keeping links with Africa. Rastafarians often have long hair called "dreadlocks." They live mostly as farmers in the hills.

14

"We are Rastafarians."

"My name is Nzinga, and here I am with my father. Our religion is called Rastafarianism. We don't like to eat meat or drink alcohol. We also never cut our hair, just letting it grow long into what are called 'dreadlocks.'"

"I'm a Baptist and I go to church most Sundays."

"My name is Tameka and I live in Anchovy, a village near Montego Bay. I'm a Christian and a member of the Baptist Church. I go to church most Sundays. I always wear my best dress, which is this yellow one, when I go to church."

There are also some **Hindus** and **Muslims** in Jamaica. Their **ancestors** worked on the sugar plantations.

In the countryside, many people believe in ghosts. They call ghosts "duppies." Before a house is built they **sacrifice** a goat. That is supposed to keep the duppies away.

Festivals

Jamaicans love to enjoy themselves during a festival. Independence Day is an important day in August, when Jamaicans remember the day they won **independence** from Britain, August 6, 1962. On Independence Day people sing and dance. In the towns they have colorful parades and fairs in the streets.

At Christmas, some people celebrate with a festival called Junkanoo. They wear masks and costumes and play music.

Reggae Sunsplash is a music festival that is held for a week in August. Reggae groups play music all night and there are many stands selling Jamaican food and drinks. Reggae music started in the poor parts of Kingston and it now sells millions of records around the world. The stadium

Fire-eating is something you might see at a Jamaican carnival. The man has to be very good at it because it is dangerous.

"At Easter we eat a special fruity bun with cheese."

"I'm called Trudi and I live in Kingston. At Easter-time we always eat bun and cheese, like I'm doing here. The bun is more like a cake, though, because it's made with lots of fruit and spices, like cinnamon. It's delicious! People give buns as presents at Easter."

"We had a carnival at the end of Lent."

"My name is Philipa. We had our first carnival last year to celebrate the end of Lent. This is the costume I wore when we paraded through the streets of Kingston behind a band. Everyone had such a good time that there is going to be a carnival every year from now on."

where the Reggae Sunsplash is held is named after Bob Marley. He died in 1981, but he is still the most famous reggae star in the world.

Homes

People like to sit in the shade outside their homes when it is hot.

In the countryside, the poorer houses are made of bamboo and wood with **corrugated iron** roofs. They are often painted in bright colors and have **verandahs** at the front. A verandah gives shelter from the sun and rain, and catches any breeze to keep the house cool. In the hills, many houses do not have electricity, and people cook on oil stoves or wood fires instead.

Wealthy families have very fine houses set in large grounds. Some of these houses used to belong to the British families who owned the huge sugar plantations.

Parts of the city of Kingston are very crowded, and homes are made out of anything people can find, like pieces of wood or sheets of plastic. Children play outside, and washing and cooking are done in the open air. These poor areas are called shanty towns. Well-to-do families usually live in the **suburbs** at the edge of the town, where there is more space.

"You have to walk to our house because the track is too narrow for a car."

"My name is Nzinga. Here I am with my parents at the front door of our house. We live in a small village near Port Antonio. You have to walk to the house because the track is too narrow for a car. On the way you pass vegetables and fruit, like coconuts and bananas, growing in our fields."

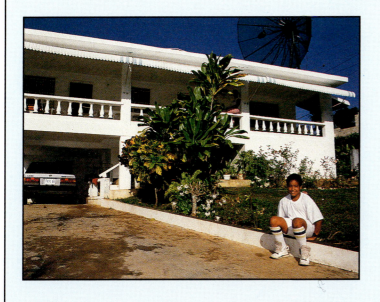

"We've got a pool and satellite TV."

"I'm Miguel, and this is my home in Ocho Rios. On the roof you can just see the huge satellite dish for getting shows from American TV. My favorite ones are on the children's channel. We've also got a swimming pool and a big yard for our dogs."

Sports and pastimes

The most popular sports in Jamaica are **cricket** and soccer. These games are played anywhere. Sometimes children play cricket on a straight piece of road using a board as the bat and an orange for the ball. The **West Indies** cricket team is one of the best in the world. When they play, everyone tunes in to listen to the match on the radio.

There is plenty to do at the beach. Some people sit and chat under a tree on the sand. If they have a guitar or a drum they may sing some of their favorite songs. When it

Jamaicans love to watch the West Indies cricket team when they play a match.

gets too hot, they can go swimming to cool down.

Playing **dominoes** is a popular pastime. Jamaicans take dominoes seriously and a game can be very exciting. Many people will gather outside a house or in a town square to watch a game.

"I'm learning to play the violin and piano."

"My name is Adrianne and I live in Mandeville. After school I go to classes to learn to play the violin and the piano. I'm the one second from the right. I've been learning the violin for a year now, but I think I'm better at the piano."

"We all swim in our pool after school."

"My name is Miguel, and this is our swimming pool. It's hot enough to swim in it all year round. After school my friends often come over and we swim in the pool. Sometimes we have races, or just play in the pool all afternoon."

Food

Breadfruit with curry sauce is a delicious take-out meal in Jamaica.

Jamaicans eat lots of vegetables and fruit because meat is expensive. Mango and paw paw are fruits that can be eaten straight from a tree. A breadfruit is a bit like a potato, and it is delicious after it has been roasted on a fire.

Jamaicans like to use spices and peppers when they cook meat or fish. They often eat beans and rice, sometimes with meat, but they are also good to eat on their own.

Akee and saltfish is Jamaica's national dish. It tastes like fishy scrambled eggs. Akee is the seed of a tropical tree, and its shell has to be broken to let out a poisonous gas before it is cooked.

"I'm choosing my lunch at a 'jerk stall.'"

"My name is Mark, and I live in Mandeville. My cousin and I are choosing our lunch at a 'jerk stall.' They're found all over Jamaica. Bits of pork and chicken, covered with a thick, spicy sauce, are cooked on a barbecue at these stalls. I'm not sure where they get their name from, though."

"Lollipops are my favorite candy at the moment."

"I'm called Yannique, which is an old French name. Here I am visiting the best place in Port Antonio. It's the candy stand at the bus station! You can buy all sorts of candy here, but my favorites at the moment are lollipops."

If they are thirsty, Jamaicans may drink sugar-cane juice. Coconut milk is also refreshing. When you cut the top off a coconut you can drink the milk right out of the shell.

Shopping

In the countryside, the village stores are small, so sometimes people have to go to a big town like Montego Bay. The towns have a bigger range of stores, so country people go there to buy clothes, furniture or electrical goods. In Kingston there are **department stores** selling many different things.

In the towns, some people buy their food in supermarkets, but most like to shop in the vegetable and spice markets. Women come from the villages to the towns to sell their goods at the markets. There are no

Food markets are very colorful because there are so many different fresh fruits and vegetables for sale.

fixed prices, and people **barter** to get the best price. The markets may also sell clothes and handicrafts, so both tourists and local people like to shop there.

"I'm helping my mother in the supermarket."

"My name is Mark. I'm helping my mother to do some shopping in a supermarket in Mandeville, where we live. You can buy fresh fruit and vegetables here, as well as frozen things and packaged and canned food."

"The outdoor market sells big, juicy tomatoes."

"I am Yannique. Here I am choosing some tomatoes at the outdoor market in Port Antonio. They're big and juicy and were grown in the countryside by the woman who is sitting on the stool. On her land she grows many other vegetables and fruit, which she brings to the market every day."

Transportation

Getting around in the big towns is easy in Jamaica. There are lots of buses and taxis. A train runs once a day across the island from Kingston to Montego Bay, and the trip takes five hours. For more money, people can fly by airplane in just twenty minutes.

There are also plenty of buses and minibuses near the coast. It is more difficult to travel in the middle of the island because the land is hilly. The roads are bumpy and they wind up and down between the hills.

Flying in a small private airplane is a new way to travel across Jamaica, if you have a lot of money.

26

Instead of waiting at bus stops Jamaicans stand on the roadside and wave the bus down. When they want to get out they shout, "One stop!" to the driver. Many of the minibuses play loud music. They are often packed with people, especially on market days and before church on Sundays.

"I ride my father's ten-speed racer."

"I'm Brian and I'm from Negril. Here I am with my father's ten-speed racing bike, which he lets me ride. I can go very fast on it, but I have to be careful because our roads are full of big holes and people drive fast and badly."

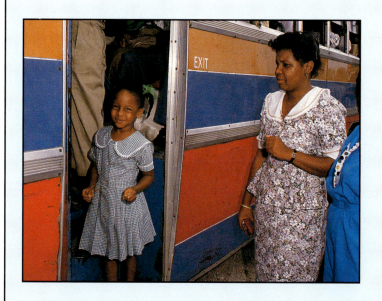

"The buses are so crowded and noisy."

"I am Yannique. When our car breaks down, my mother and I have to use the local bus to get home. We don't like doing this because the buses are so crowded and noisy. Sometimes you cannot even get on them and have to wait for the next one."

Let's discuss Jamaica

Now that you know a little about Jamaica and its people, can you see any differences between how you live and how Jamaican children live? Do you ever have to do chores when you come home from school?

Christians like Tameka like to wear their best clothes to church on Sundays. When do you like to dress up to look your best?

Music and dancing are very important to Jamaicans, especially during a festival. Do you celebrate festivals with music?

Some children like Yannique like to go to the vegetable market. Do you ever go shopping in a market?

This is a statue of Bob Marley. Jamaicans like to remember him because he helped to make their culture known around the world.

The tourism industry in Jamaica makes a lot of money, but not all the money stays with Jamaicans. Many of the hotels are owned by foreign companies. What problems might this cause?

Big hotels are built next to beaches as more tourists visit the island.

These banners are advertising reggae dances in Montego Bay. Reggae music is popular all over Jamaica.

Glossary

Ancestors People far back in a family's history.

Baptist The Protestant sect (group) to which many Jamaicans belong.

Barter To bargain over how much to pay for something.

Bauxite A type of rock from which aluminum is made.

Capital The city where the government of a country is based.

Christians Followers of Jesus Christ.

Coral A hard substance made up of the skeletons of tiny sea animals.

Corrugated iron Sheet iron that has been given a wavy surface to make it stronger.

Cricket A team game played with a ball, bats and wicket.

Culture The ideas and arts that make a particular group of people different from other groups.

Department store A large store that has many sections selling different goods.

Dominoes A game played by matching the spots on oblong pieces.

Harvest To pick or gather crops.

Hindus People who follow the main religion of India.

Hurricanes Extremely strong winds that can destroy buildings.

Independence Freedom from control by others.

Mine To dig something out of the earth.

Muslims People who follow the Islamic religion.

Plantation A large area of land that is used for growing one type of crop, such as sugar cane.

Reggae A type of pop music with a strong beat, which is very popular in the West Indies.

Roman Catholic The branch of the Christian Church headed by the Pope.

Rum A strong alcoholic drink made from sugar cane.

Sacrifice To give something as an offering to a god.

Souvenir An item to keep as a reminder of a place or event.

Suburb An area of houses at the edge of a town.

Tourists People who visit a place on vacation.

Tropical Of or in the tropics, the areas just north and south of the equator, which have very hot weather all year round.

Verandah A porch with a roof.

West Indies The group of islands in the Atlantic, between North and South America, including the Bahamas and the Antilles. Jamaica is in the Antilles.

Books to read

Hubley, John and Penny Hubley. *A Family in Jamaica.* Minneapolis, MN: Lerner Publications, 1985.

Jamaica in Pictures. Minneapolis, MN: Lerner Publications, 1987.

Lye, Keith. *Take a Trip to Jamaica.* New York: Franklin Watts, 1988.

Wilkins, Frances. *Jamaica.* New York: Chelsea House, 1988.

Picture acknowledgments

All photographs by David Cumming except page 22, Hutchison Library (John Wright). Maps on contents page and page 5 by Jenny Hughes.

Index

Acknowledgments

The photographer would like to thank the following: Audrey Anderson and Jacqueline Goldson of the Jamaica Tourist Board, Joy Worton and Hope Stewart in Kingston, Diana McIntyre-Pike and the staff of the Hotel Astra in Mandeville and Ian Gordon, for their help on this project. The author would like to thank Philippa Sharp and May Pen for seeking out some useful information for this book.